AF374810

LET'S TALK, EMERGENCIES!

A GUIDE TO LIFE-SAVING LESSONS
IN KID-FRIENDLY LANGUAGE

Written by
Cheryl Daley

Illustrations by
Cheryl Crouthamel

Losing a child is undoubtedly the hardest
journey there is, one that no parent
should have to endure.

To those who have:
Your pain is seen. Your child is remembered.

Your strength amazes.

This book is dedicated to you.

-C. Daley-

Knowing your shapes, colors, and letters,
your numbers and even your sounds,
are all important skills to learn,
as you grow leaps and bounds.

But another thing we should discuss,
that's more important, you see,
is what you can do to keep yourself safe,
if there's an emergency.

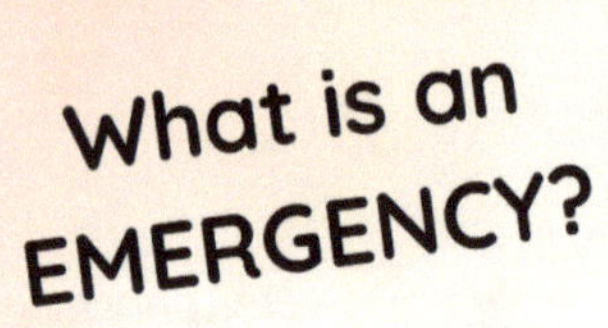

An emergency is a serious, unexpected,
and sometimes dangerous situation
that needs quick action,
and often the help of others!

What are some things
you might consider
to be an emergency?

Step ONE is knowing what to do,
you might feel a bit scared!
I'll show you how you can get help
so you will feel prepared.

9-1-1 are the numbers to press
on any phone to call
an ambulance, fire truck or the police.
That number does it all!

Let's practice saying "9-1-1" together!
"9-1-1"
"9-1-1"

But which one is the nine, you say?
It's easy to mix with a six!
The nine is the one that has a big head
and a body as thin as a stick!

Then you press the number one
and then you press it again.
Send your call and listen for help.
You can do it, I know that you can!

Let's practice calling 9-1-1 here!

If using a cell phone, don't forget to press the green circle to send the call!

1
2 ABC
3 DEF
4 GHI
5 JKL
6 MNO
7 PQRS
8 TUV
9 WXYZ
*
0 +
#

Our phones can come in different types,
like a landline or a cell phone.
A landline stays plugged into the wall
and a cell, you can take on the go!

But a cell can lock, the screen goes black
the numbers just aren't there to press!
Did you know you can still dial 9-1-1?
Let's slowly go through the steps.

We can practice with a real phone or use these pictures!
The steps for calling 9-1-1 from a locked cell phone may look like this:
#1
#2
or

Hold both buttons for 3 seconds

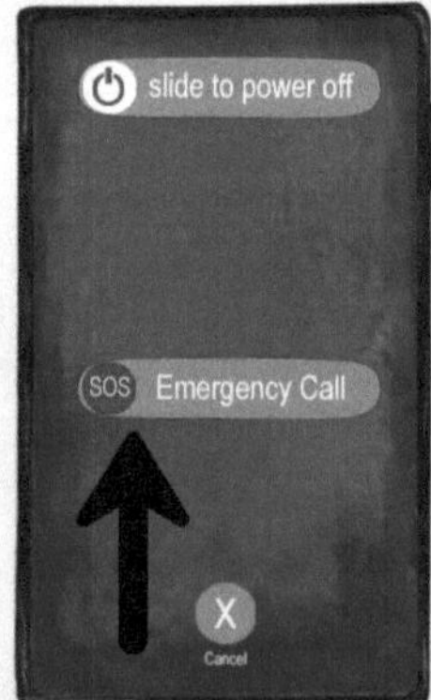

slide to power off
SOS Emergency Call
X
Cancel
Swipe over

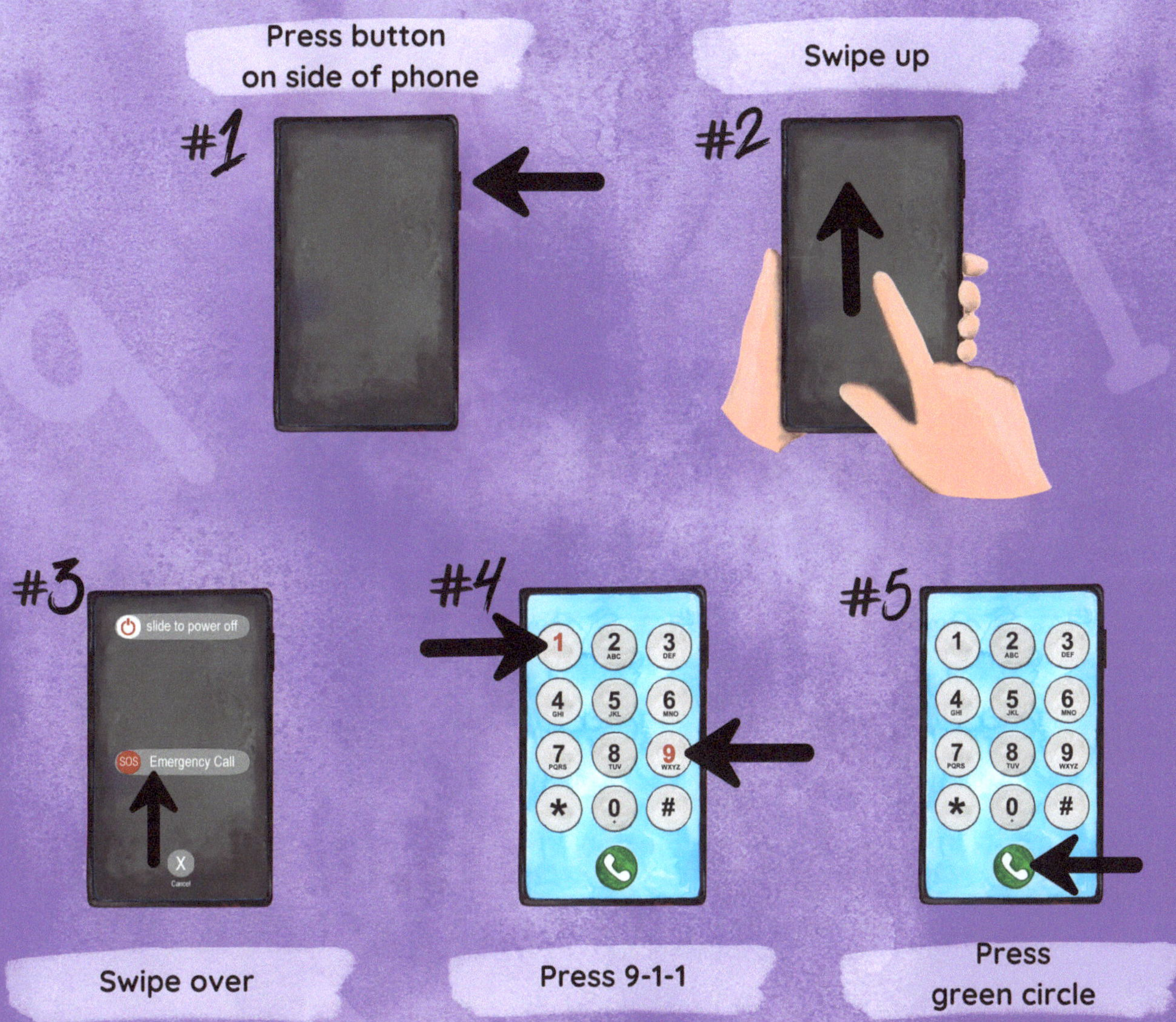

Please remember that you should only call
9-1-1 when you have an emergency!

9-1-1 Dispatch will come on the line,
"How can we help?" they will ask.
Say why you've called and give them your name.
They'll need both your FIRST and your LAST.

"9-1-1.."

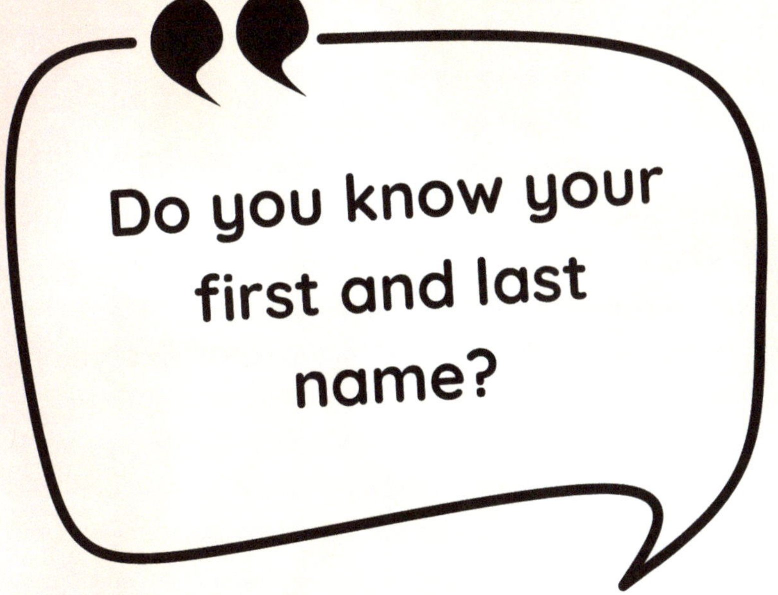

Do you know your first and last name?
Let's practice it now!

Now that you've practiced your first and last name,
do you know what else Mommy goes by?
Both Daddy and Momma have real names, as well.
You should learn them, and I'll tell you why!

If you're lost, there are tools
to find Mom and Dad,
but to use them
you need information.

An address, a number
or first and last name,
will all help you
to find their location.

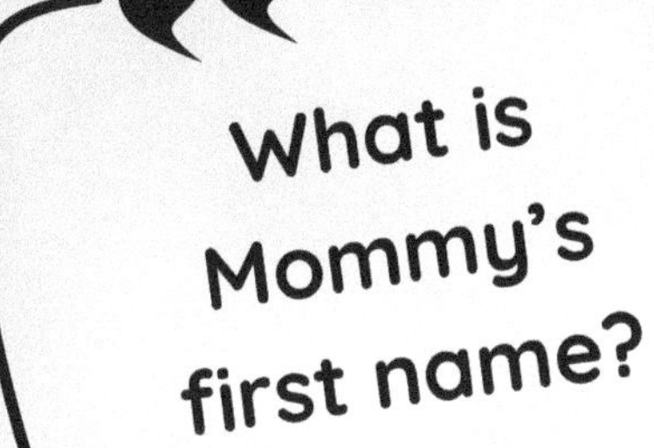

What is Mommy's first name?
And what's Mommy's last name?
What about Daddy? Do you know his first and last name?

Next, 9-1-1 Dispatch will ask where you live,
or "What's your address?" they might say.
Both mean the same and what they want to know
is, "How can we FIND YOU today?"

AMBULANCE

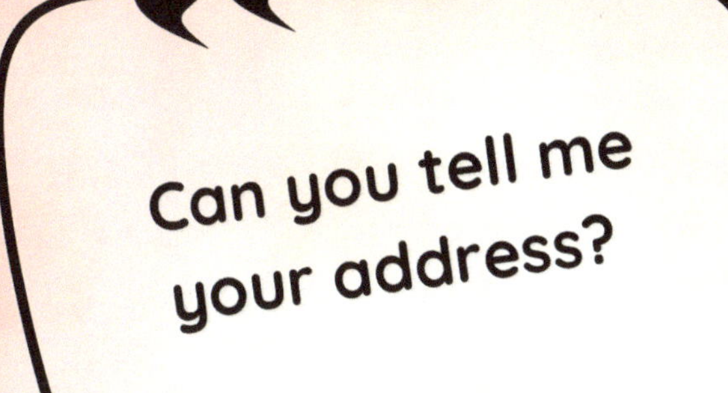
Can you tell me your address?

What if I ask, "Where do you live?"

It's okay if it's hard to remember your address! With practice, it will get easier!

Another skill that's important to learn
is how to call Mom or Dad.
If you're lost or hurt, or at a friend's house
and find yourself feeling sad.

Learning these numbers will be tough at first,
but with practice you'll know them by heart!
Your parents will be just a phone call away
whenever you are apart!

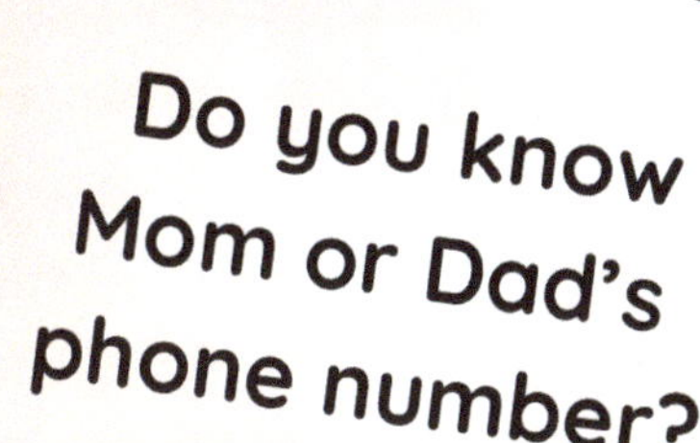

Do you know
Mom or Dad's
phone number?

Let's practice
dialing it now!

1
2
ABC
3
DEF
4
GHI
5
JKL
6
MNO
7
PQRS
8
TUV
9
WXYZ
*
0
+
#

But there may come a time when you can't find a phone,
so finding a neighbor will do.
Let's talk now about the people you trust,
and what neighbor you would go to.

What is
TRUST?
Trust is
the belief in someone
to always tell you the truth
and protect you from danger.

Is there a neighbor you trust
that you can go to
in an emergency?

What if that neighbor lives over the road?
Be smart if you're crossing the street!

Look RIGHT, LEFT, RIGHT
to make sure there's no cars,
and don't run or you'll trip on your feet.

We've learned the numbers for 9-1-1,
our address, and our phone.
But what would you do if you wake up and smell
a whole lot of smoke in your home?

You might hear the sound, it goes "BEEP, BEEP, BEEP!"
The alarm is saying, "Get Out!"
Let's plan what to do if there is a fire,
we all need a safe escape route!

If you see a clear path out your window or door,
get out as soon as you can!
Is there a spot that your family will meet?
Go there, just like we planned!

But suppose you cannot escape from your room,
it's hot or the smoke is too thick.
Stay low to the ground, but please DO NOT HIDE-
so the firemen can find you, and quick!

Fire can help us in so many ways
but it's also a danger, it's true.

If one of its flames should land on your clothes,
listen to what you must do:

STOP where you are and DROP to the ground,
then ROLL yourself all about.
Yes—
"Stop, Drop and Roll" are the steps to remember
and "FIRE!" is what you should shout!

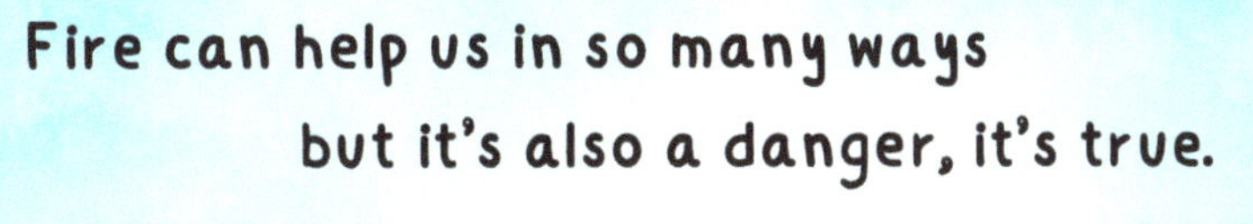

Where is your
meeting spot
if there is a fire?

What would you do
if you or your clothes
are on fire?

"STOP!"
"DROP!"
"and ROLL!"

Now let's discuss how to act around water;
in the bath, at the pool, or a lake.
When you scrub-a-dub dub, remain calm in the tub,
and use care with each step that you take.

For water outside, stay far from the edge.
Just an inch can be dangerous, you know?
Do not goof around because you could slip,
and into the water, you'll go!

Some water is deeper than it might look,
and that pool cover might not be tight!
Get an adult if you want to swim
and be sure that you stay in their sight.

Now on we'll go, just a couple more things,
that's if you're up to the task!
What do you do if a stranger approaches?
Well, I'm glad that you asked!

You know how Mom always says to be nice,
and keep your manners in line?
BUT if a stranger is wanting YOUR help,
it's better you're careful than kind.

While folks are mostly warmhearted and good,
there are bad things that some people do.
You can't trust someone that you don't really know,
they may not be telling the truth.

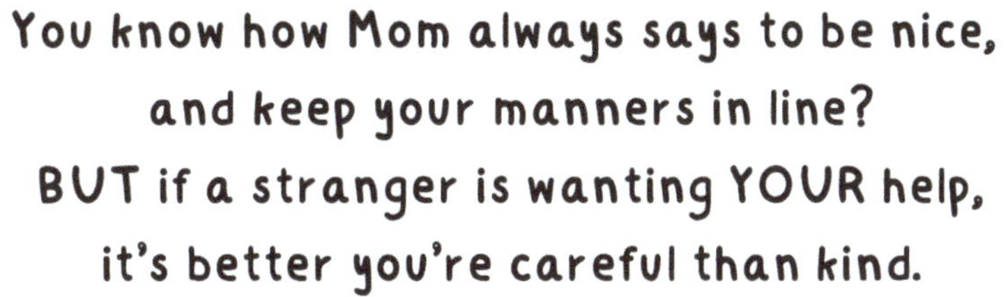

So run and find Mom— or run and find Dad.
Your safety is *PRIORITY!*
Tell them a stranger's in need of their help.
Wow, what a HERO you'll be!

But strangers are not always somewhere outside,
they can chat through your tablet or phone.
Please don't be scared, but I need you aware
if you're on the internet alone.

If someone online says, "Hey, let's meet up,"
or offers you something you want,
please do not trust that they're telling the truth.
Run and tell Daddy or Mom.

Same goes for someone who tells you a secret,
and wants you to keep it for them.
A secret should not make you hurt, sad, or scared.
If it does, they're not really your friend.

If this ever happens, you must tell your parents.
A teacher can be of help, too.
Remember that you should always feel safe,
a secret should never hurt you.

As you get older, you'll start to see,
your responsibilities will grow.
Like switching to a booster seat
when in the car, we go.

Your seatbelt must stay over your chest
and not tucked under your arm.
It's your job to follow this rule
when riding around in a car.

Now for a BIGGIE! When playing with friends,
toys like Nerf guns are always big fun.
But please don't confuse the foam bullets they use,
for the ones that are in a real gun.

If you see a gun, remember DON'T TOUCH!
Leave and search 'til a grown-up is found.
This shows me you're responsible, you see—
harm will come if you're messing around.

There are so many ways we can learn to stay safe,
that it starts to feel heavy—I know.
But little by little, we'll talk it all through,
and one day soon, you'll be a PRO!

It's rare that you'll ever need all these tips.
Preparing is just smart to do.
And maybe one day, you'll discover that you
want to HELP in emergencies, TOO!

Additional Information for Parents:

When should I call 911?

Reasons to call 911 include, but are not limited to:

- Life threatening situations
- Fires
- Motor vehicle accidents
- Injuries requiring medical attention
- Hazardous chemical spills
- Smoke detector, carbon monoxide alarm or other alarms sounding
- Smoke in a building
- If you see someone hurting someone else
- To get help for someone who is hurt
- If you see someone taking something that belongs to someone else or breaking into a home or business

When not to call 911:

Calling 911 as a joke or knowing that an emergency situation does not exist is a crime and subject to prosecution. If you call 911 to see if it is working, stay on the line and advise the operator you are just testing.

Non-emergency situations, including:

- For information
- For directory assistance
- For your injured or lost pet
- Abandoned vehicles
- Asking for directions
- Parking complaints
- Questions about tickets, warrants, court dates, etc.

What if I need police or fire assistance, but it's not an emergency?

You should call the non-emergency number for your local police department.

What if I call 911 in error?

Don't Hang up! Stay on the line and advise the dispatcher that you dialed in error. If you hang up, the following will happen:
A call back to the phone is initiated by the dispatcher to determine if there is an emergency. If the dispatcher is unable to contact the caller to verify that there is no emergency, a law enforcement emergency response unit is dispatched to the residence to determine if an emergency situation exists. The operator would prefer to talk to an adult in these instances. If the dispatcher makes contact and still feels there may be a problem, the officer will continue to the location to verify there is no emergency

Can Alexa call 911 for me?

No, Alexa can't directly call 911 on a cell phone due to communication laws, but there are some workarounds:

Emergency Assist

This feature connects users with an agent who can alert emergency services on their behalf. To use Emergency Assist, say "Alexa, call for help". The agent can send first responders, relay important information like home address and medications, and notify up to 25 emergency contacts. To set up Emergency Assist, open the Alexa app, tap More, and select Alexa Emergency Assist.

Will Siri call 911 if asked?

Yes. The simple command, "Hey Siri, dial 9-1-1," will do exactly that. And you do have three seconds to hit the Cancel button before the call is placed.

Will Google Assistant call 911?

While Google Assistant cannot call 911 by default, a Nest Aware subscription enables it within the Google Home app on your phone.

Around the house tips:
• If you do not have a landline phone, consider adding one to your home. Your child will always know where the phone is located, and you never have to worry about the phone being out of battery. Check with your cable provider, local phone service, or a company like Ooma to find out what is available in your area.

• You can purchase a home phone with picture inserts on the speed dial buttons. Program 9-1-1, a parent, or grandparent to the speed dial buttons and add their photo, so your child can easily get help in an emergency.

• Identify your nearest hospital and the quickest route to get there. Practice the route by taking a ride there and seeing where the emergency entrance is. Is there valet parking or a parking lot close by? Knowing these facts before an emergency happens is key!

• Take a CPR course and contact your pediatrician for further safety information

• For crib safety, do not allow curtains or string from blinds to be anywhere near the crib. Do not hang anything over or within reach of the crib.
In loving memory of Violet R.

For assistance in locating the hidden numbers within the illustrations, head to www.cheryldaley.com

To reinforce the concepts in this book,
don't forget to grab the
LET'S TALK, EMERGENCIES!
Activity Book!

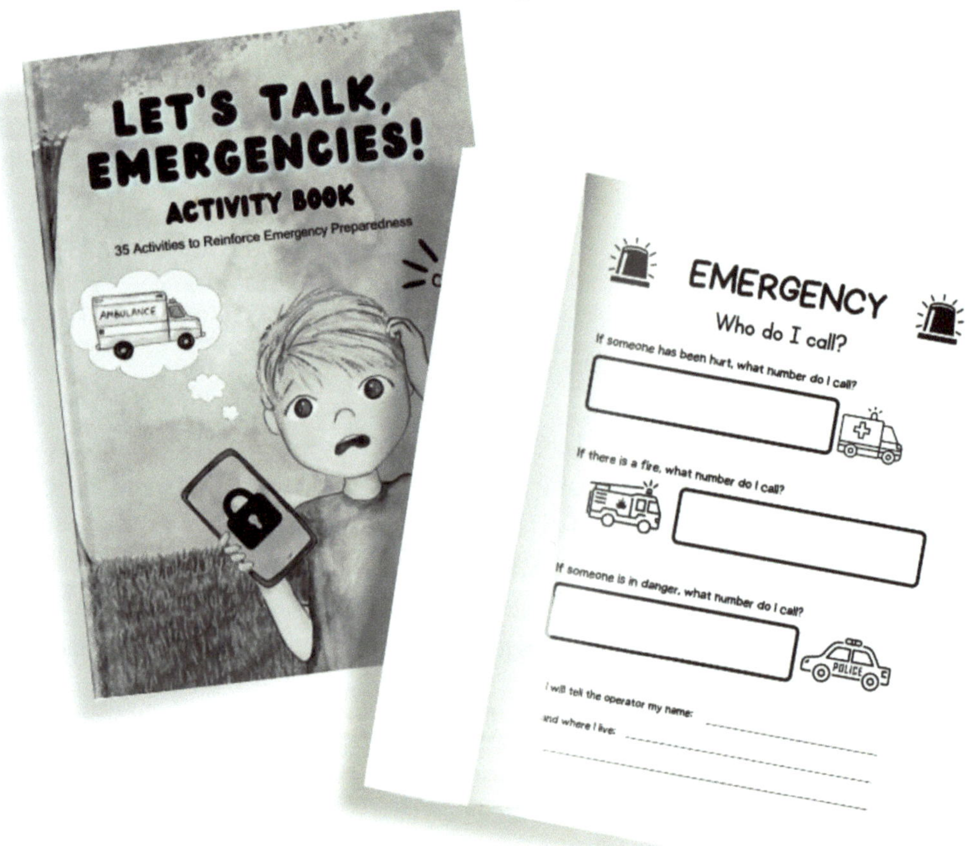

Available on
Amazon
OR
WWW.CHERYLDALEY.COM

Meet the Cheryls!

Cheryl Daley, author of Let's Talk, Emergencies! is a wife and mother of two. After 16 years of government work, Cheryl left her job to homeschool her children. Cheryl also has a podcast, The Homeschool How To, where she interviews homeschooling families to learn all the ways homeschooling can be done.

Cheryl's passions have shifted from being a career woman to being a stay-at-home mom, immersing herself in learning, alongside her children, all about nature and self-sufficiency. She invites you to join her on her journey by following her Instagram page, @TheHomeschoolHowToPodcast and checking out her podcast, The Homeschool How To, if homeschooling is something on your heart. More of Cheryl's work can be found at www.cheryldaley.com

Cheryl Crouthamel is the illustrator of Let's Talk, Emergencies! After retiring from the NYPD, Cheryl decided to start her own freelance illustration business. While raising three kids with her husband and illustrating over fifty books and publications over the last eighteen years, Cheryl loves exactly what she does each and every day from her cozy home studio in Northern NJ. You can find her current work at www.cherylcroutart.com

If you found this book helpful in any way, PLEASE take a moment to scan here and leave us a review!
It would mean SO much! - Thank you!!